THE YOUNG PROFESSIONAL'S
GUIDE TO MAKING
AN IMPACT

MONTAZ MCCRAY

GP
GREENFIELD PUBLICATIONS

Published by Godzchild Publications
a division of Godzchild, Inc.
22 Halleck St., Newark, NJ 07104
www.godzchildproductions.net

Printed in the United States of America 2022 - 1st Edition

Library of Congress Cataloging-in-Publications Data
The Young Professional's Guide to Making an Impact

ISBN-13 978-1-937391-75-1

1. Montaz 2. McCray

2022

Montaz built his business on being **reliable, diligent and assertive** when helping clients buy and sell real estate. He has proven that he can be innovative and creative in order make sure his clients win.

Montaz will listen to you, make sure he understands your needs and wants. He will work tirelessly to make sure you achieve your goals. To him, it is not about the numbers in the transaction it is about the people.

Graduating top in his class from Goucher college with a degree in accounting proves to be an asset for his clients.

Montaz has helped 35 families achieve their real estate goals in 2021. He is in the top 10% of Keller Williams Realty Centre agents.

Member of the KW Sports & Entertainment Network.

Montaz has such an amazing work ethic and client interaction model the VP of Training for Keller Williams Realty International, James Shaw interviewed him for all Keller Williams agents to learn from his stellar business model.

TABLE OF
Contents

ACKNOWLEDGEMENTS

I would like to acknowledge my Mother, Father, Sister and family for their continued support and prayers. I love and appreciate them for always meeting me where I'm at while trying to build a career, it's not always easy, but they are always there for me. Then also any mentors for pouring into me relentlessly and helping me advance my career by sharing valuable experiences with me. Lastly, I couldn't be here without my clients who are constantly supporting me and referring me business which means the world to myself and my family.

CHAPTER 1

Give It Your All

"Fall seven times. Stand up Eight."
—*Japanese Proverb*

My name is Montaz McCray and this is my story. Let me warn you. My story is not a conventional story. My story isn't even a predictable story. Most mentors I admire, both near and far, have mind-blowing experiences that changed everything for them. They landed the perfect job after college. They ended up on the same elevator as a multi-millionaire. They were raised in the hood and had no parents to guide them. They went from rags to riches in minutes and experienced record-breaking revenue overnight.

Well, that's not me.

None of those stories describe my journey.

I didn't start out in real estate winning. In fact, when I changed careers, I experienced a 5-month drought where I didn't sell anything at all! Once I started closing on deals, the properties were all relatively low, considering the area where I live. My first closing was only $60,000. That was the cost of the entire property and left me little room for profit. It was a crazy milestone but a necessary one. For five long months, I contemplated quitting at least five times a day. For five long months, I sought advice from people who told me that I should've stayed at my corporate job. After all, I was making six figures. I graduated at the top of my class, and I earned a 3.7 cumulative GPA in college.

My mom loved the fact that I had landed a dream job in corporate America, and she advised me to stick it out until something actually "hit." But something within me could not settle. Something within me knew that there was more for me outside of this comfortable 9-5, and for some people, their greatest dreams will come true inside of their corporate management position. For me, the office felt like I was living inside of a box. It was too small for me. I couldn't breathe. I couldn't relax. I couldn't lean into my expertise because I was constantly plagued by this truth—"there is always more on the other side of safe."

Maybe you're reading this book and you have always lived a safe life. Maybe safety and security have been best friends for you. Maybe you've done a pretty good job with the relationships you've garnered, and the revenue you've earned. And if that's working for you, hey, listen, I'm not here to tell you to do what I've done. But I am here to tell you—there's more. Regardless of the decisions you make after reading my story, I hope you will not allow the comfortability of a predictable paycheck to keep you from pursuing your dreams.

I have always been an outgoing person. I have always experienced immense joy talking to people and finding out more about their passions. In my corporate job, my social interactions were limited, and I hated that. In my corporate job, I saw and heard people complain about the work demands that kept them from enjoying life, taking a vacation, and building a legacy. I wanted a life that I never had to take a vacation from. I wanted a career that supported my self-care goals. I didn't want to drag into work on Monday and only live for the weekends. Life is too short to spend the majority of your life unhappy and unfulfilled. I decided to do an unpopular thing—I decided to give it my all.

Are You Giving It Your All?

Let me ask you something:

What are your dreams?

What are your goals?

Are you giving it your all right now? Or are you splitting your focus between making someone else's dreams come true and honoring your own?

This is what I know for sure—when your focus is split, your energy is split, too. Many people will tell you that multi-tasking is a core trait that every businessowner needs to have. But I believe commitment to giving your dreams all your attention (and not just some of it) is the greatest skill a businessowner can have. What would it look like to give your dreams the best of your energy, and not the crumbs you have left? What would it look like to prioritize YOU?

Some people work a 9-5 to pay bills for a season. I get that. But don't turn a season into a century. You should always have an exit plan. You should always have an Option B or C so that you can do what you believe you've been placed in the earth to do. If not, you will be frustrated, disappointed, and filled with regret. If not, people will create distance between you and your obligations because no one wants to be around someone who is sad all the time. But there is another way. Giving it your all will come with a high price tag but let me tell you the truth-it was worth every penny!

PAY THE PRICE FOR PERSONAL JOY

I am so glad I decided to pay the price for personal joy. I am now, currently, giving my all and experiencing great moments in business that I would've never experienced playing it safe. In giving it your all, prepare to disappoint those who love you (even if they don't understand you). But at the same time, do what's best for you, even if you make mistakes and missteps. On the other side of focus is a reward that will bring you satisfaction, fulfilment, and peace.

As stated earlier, I graduated from college in November of 2020. I remember it vividly because my undergraduate course work ended around Thanksgiving (and who doesn't remember good food from thanksgiving!) In any case, my degree is in Business with a specialization in accounting and finance. I got my first job in the DC area. My mom was overjoyed because I graduated at the top of my class AND I landed a lucrative position working for an accounting firm in DC. At the same time, I decided to obtain my real estate's license and I became super busy. I was already studying for my final exams for school, so I thought, "What's one more exam? Let's pile it on now and benefit later." With that decision, I completed and passed my real estate exams and then started my job during the same month that I had received my real estate license.

About 3 months into my accounting job, they let me go. They fired me because they thought my real estate career was a conflict of interest. I wasn't performing well (in their minds) and I get it—I had put a lot of time into real estate. But who could blame me? Real estate was a part of my destiny. School gave me the tools. The firm gave me a job. But I needed TIME, FREEDOM, and LIMITLESSNESS!

Once my mind gets fixated on something, it's hard for me to split my focus. So, yea, I got fired in March of

2021 and I sold nothing for 5 months. Can you imagine how devastating that was? I'm sure you can imagine it because we all have stories that pushed us out of our comfort zone. Everyone has a "breaking point" that produces a decision to give it your all. My first closing happened in April of that same year, and I made about $1400 from it.

Truthfully, I questioned everything in April. I think I had a true encounter with a legit identity crisis. I felt like an imposter. I felt like a person who presented all of this positivity and optimism, but my bank account didn't support anything I believed. I had to sit down and ask myself, "Am I really who I claim to be?" Did it make sense to leave a job making $100,000 a year only to end up with a $1400 return? But trouble don't last always! The firing from that job lit a fire inside of me.

I don't know if I would've grinded as hard if I hadn't gotten fired. And many of you are reading this and can relate to the hard times I'm talking about. What if that hard time was a "fire" that lit a "fire" within you? What if you needed that level of disappointment to finally step out and do it? This is what I learned in 2021. First, I learned that I am built to win. Whenever I set my mind on something, I do it. Second, I learned that dreams don't come true until you're willing to jump. *Remember when you learned how to swim? Remember when you took your first big dive off the swimming board? Remember when you finally submitted that application? Remember when you applied for the house, or took a chance at love? Sometimes you must jump for your dreams and be willing to leave the safety net. What are your personal or professional safety nets? Is it living in an affordable property you are renting? Is it staying in a toxic work environment? Is it asking other people for loans until you can figure out your process and path?* **The safety net is never safe; the safety net is seductive. The safety net keeps you settling. The safety net was a cushion of comfort for me, but it never helped me.**

ASK THE RIGHT QUESTIONS

Most people ask me "What did I leave" after hearing that I walked away from that job. But that wasn't the right question. The real question was "What did I gain?" And I'm here to tell you, I gained my life back. I gained control over my schedule. I gained my grind back. I gained limitless opportunities, and I gained the confidence to build from the ground up.

What will you gain once you finally take that leap? What will you gain when decide to give it your all? I gained my freedom, and I gained a life by design that I could create. For me, it was worth the risk. It was scary but it was worth it. And once I closed on one property, I found my niche and kept on winning. In 7 months, I closed on $11.5 million in real estate. In 7 months, I learned how to build a bullet-proof business. In 7 months, I mastered the art of learning scripts and strategies to achieve high ranking sales. It was painful getting started, but it would've been more painful to never start.

Many times, I was told no. Many times, I experienced humiliation. In fact, when my job fired me, they locked me out of my office. Can you imagine? And when I started closing deals, I also hosted open houses that no one showed up for. Because I am committed to telling you the truth throughout this entire book, there is something I need to share with you. Sometimes you can give it your all and things still won't go your way. Sometimes you will advise a client to the best of your ability, but the deal will fall through for a reason that's completely out of your control. In life, I have learned there will be many things out of your control that will directly influence you, however just because it doesn't go your way doesn't mean you should quit. I've seen and experienced it all in my real estate career, and that's why I decided to write this book. I didn't want to wait another year without bringing you into the truth. You can do this. You may not decide to sell homes, and you may not want to go the route I chose, but I know you have it in you to win. I want you to keep reading so that you can learn how to fail forward. I want you to gain the resilience necessary to soar even after you stall. Just promise me that no matter what happens, that you will give it your all.

Just give it your all.

CHAPTER 2

Forward Thinking: Having A Next Level Mindset

"Big ideas come from forward thinking people who challenge the norm, think outside the box, and invent the world they see inside rather than submitting to the limitations of current dilemmas."

—*Bishop T.D. Jakes*

More often than not, you may have heard that people will enter the world of real estate solely to make money. Yes, real estate can be very lucrative. However, unless you're extremely lucky, it's not immediate. There are essential tools that you need to have handy and know how to use. You also have to be creative and be willing to take the risk of innovation as your presented with new opportunities. As I previously mentioned, I didn't start off winning. Remember, my first closing was $60,000. If I didn't know or believe in myself, I would have given up right then and there. As a matter of fact, a lot of people do. According to real estate educator Tom Ferry, between 87-90% of realtors give up within their first year. I had to believe in my potential and learn how to be a real estate professional. I had to form a habit of forward thinking and develop a mindset to sustain the habit.

You may be thinking, *But Montaz, where do I even start?*

I'm glad you asked.

Let's take a look at some of the problems that realtors often experience in their first year.

COMMON MISTAKES NEW AGENTS MAKE

1. Lack of leads – Building a pool of potential clients can be extremely difficult for a realtor just starting out. Many new real estate agents rely on friends, family, or other connections to create their lead network. The problem is that this approach and the people in it can be exhausted really fast. Therefore, you need to get out of your comfort zone by door knocking and consistently hosting open houses.

2. Time – Real estate requires a lot. As a field that thrives on investments, one of the largest investments that a new realtor will make is their time. The initial step is to go through the process of obtaining licensure in the state(s) they plan on selling homes in. States have particular

requirements as to how many hours are required in order to obtain the necessary licenses.

Time management is also essential. While not impossible, it is impractical to treat real estate as a part time job because it requires full time work. Many hours will be spent marketing, showing homes, or filling out paperwork among other things. Weekends may be lost and workdays can be long. Even the ability to create hours varies depending on what is realistic for one's personal life and what they're trying to accomplish in the real estate market.

Patience is also key. There are going to be days where things move slower than frozen molasses. As the saying goes, *trust the process.* Impatience can rob a new realtor of the fruits of their efforts. Reason being? The harmful assumption that something doesn't work if it doesn't yield an immediate result. You wouldn't expect a pizza to be fully baked when you just put it in the oven, right? Neither would you expect a seed to grow into a tree after it was just planted. A realtor has to be just as willing to wait as they are to push.

3. Work Ethic – This is what tends to make or break a lot of realtors. Real estate is a realm of competition. It's easy to become discouraged when you see

others thriving. It's easy to slip up when you try to attempt to do what others are doing in order to thrive. Everyone's process will be different. Realtors work in different areas, with different budgets, different clientele, etc. Approaching real estate with a broad paintbrush is what causes a lot of realtors to mismanage their journey. How are you treating leads? Are you treating them like a meal ticket or like someone who is trying to build their future? Are you listening to what they're looking for, or are you only showing them what will be the most profitable for you? Are you consistent? Are you following up? Are you being smart with your time and resources? Are you watching the market? A great work ethic means that you're taking an honest inventory of what's in front of you and adjusting as necessary.

4. Knowledge of Marketing Tools – Realtors can put themselves in a corner if they are unaware of or unwilling to use various efforts to generate leads. Some leads can be acquired through grassroots efforts. Some leads require a more tech savvy approach. Others come through networking events. If a realtor refuses to be flexible or doesn't research these methods, they can't develop the necessary strategies to convert those leads into

closed deals. Using a combination of tools creates a wide net and leads to a diverse catch. If you're not utilizing social media, you're more likely to miss out on reaching new leads that are not reachable by conventional methods. Social media is a great way to connected with those that are of a younger demographic or potential leads within certain income brackets. Facebook, Instagram, and Tik Tok are some of the best ways to hold virtual open houses, create events, and showcase houses that you are trying to sell.

5. Resources and Finances – The final nail in the coffin for new realtors is money. Generating income through real estate takes time. There are times where there are little to no sales, and even then, they may not always lead to an ideal profit. Money is essential for advertising, gas money, paying vendors, and more. If a realtor doesn't have the savings to cover those, there needs to be a cost-effective alternative. The problem is that most new realtors do not have the savings or the patience to research cost-effective alternatives. The best thing a new agent can do is budget. This way you can account for the expenses that you want to be immediately reimbursed for.

DOING WHAT IT TAKES TO SUCCEED

My real estate journey started like many realtors. I was working in a completely different field before I got into real estate. I was working as a staff accountant for three months when a friend of mine told me that he was getting ready to leave his job. He had worked for Apple and was doing well there. I was curious as to why he wanted to leave. Then he showed me his commission checks and that lit a spark in me. I knew that I had to put in the work in order to make the kind of money that he did. I studied hard, going above and beyond the course I was studying. I developed a laser focus on what I was doing. I studied YouTube videos. I made flashcards. I used the CE Shop website to study for the exam and moved at my own pace. I printed out and internalized test materials. I reached out to other agents and asked for guidance. All of those steps were foundational to developing the type of realtor that I wanted to become.

Once I obtained my license, I did even *more* research. I spoke to my parents. I reached out to friends of friends. Starting conversations with them not only gave me the start of my lead pool, but it also allowed me to determine what my goals were. My goal was to create a top-tier experience for my clients. I watched trainings late at night, consistently studied scripts and just focused on out working my competition to provide a higher quality service to my clientele and be more knowledgeable. I then had to cultivate the systems I would need in order to reach that goal. One caveat though; I still made the effort to use those systems even when the processes weren't fully in place. Doing so allowed me to see the parts of the system that worked and where I could improve. That meant that I had to fake it till I made it most of the time.

I started with creating a checklist to know what my clients needed. I was intentional to go to open houses in the places I wanted to sell and study my competition. I pulled comp sheets so I could thoroughly know and understand the areas where I hoped to sell. I hosted open houses even when no one showed up. I would film tours to post on social media. I practiced how to speak with leads. I learned about the furnishings that people desired for their homes and their differences. Gas stove versus electric? No problem, I could explain it. Questions about the flooring? I had the answer. I positioned myself to be as prepared as possible. My commitment showed through all the blood, sweat, and tears.

CONFIDENCE IS KEY

Being a newbie in real estate can be intimidating. As I applied myself to learning the skills to be a great and competent agent, I also took the time to become a *confident* agent. Key point, confident not *cocky*. We can all think back to a time where we've encountered a salesperson. If they lacked confidence or knowledge about what they were selling, nine times out of ten, the sale didn't go through because their demeanor made the product look bad. On the opposite end, if they were too pushy or aggressive, their behavior would turn off potential buyers before they had a chance to consider the product. The best salespeople tend to walk the middle. They know when to press and when to pull back. They effectively communicate the product and show it in an authentic and positive light. However, the driving force ends up being how they treat their customers. Smiles, warm energy, attentiveness are all signs of a confident salesperson no matter the field.

When you're confident, you don't have to be forceful or shady to land the deal. You're able to illustrate the worth of something in a way that builds a buyer's trust in you. Confidence helps to convey to a client that they are supported and they are getting the best of the best. Great customer service habits are an excellent way to build confidence because you get to hear your client's pain points. An equally important benefit of developing confidence is being able to handle rejections. As much as we'd like to, we can't win them all. Being confident allows us to not internalize a client declining as something wrong with us. We can always take what doesn't work and use it as a means to improve. This also helps us to endure when we go through stretches of no sales.

Real estate being a commission only business contributes to the mental struggle that many new realtors have. Gaps in payment can add to that mental stress. Confidence begets perseverance and wisdom, which will preserve you in the rough times. It will give you the courage to try new things and see them through. Confidence is more than an attitude, it's the step to the next level.

One of the most powerful mindset lessons I learned was from my mother. There was a time during my basketball career where I had only spent three weeks on the team because I was over it and wanted to focus on my academics. A week went by and before I knew it, I was back in front of the coach asking for my spot back. The coach did me a solid and brought me back on and I was able to finish the season. During this time my mom told me to never quit and to finish what I started.

You can never go wrong in becoming your own cheerleader. There will be times when you are the only encouragement you have. Your success and drive to prosper will bring out the worst in people. When those times come, you have to remember that ultimately you are doing this for you. Everything that you have endured to get to this point is worth it. You are creating a legacy that you are worthy of, and you need to see it through. Tempting as it is, don't quit. Finish what you started and see where the audacity to continue to will take you.

CHAPTER 3
Learning To Lead The Leads

"If people like you, they'll listen to you, but if they trust you, they'll do business with you."
—*Zig Ziglar*

Now that we've unpacked where a lot of agents struggle, it's now time to build up your arsenal. Take a moment to put yourself in the seat of your prospect. Think about their common frustrations. What patterns do you typically see? Does it have to do with their income? Does it have to do with the location where they're seeking to buy a home? Are they not finding the accommodations that they're looking for? These questions are an excellent starting point to having stellar customer service and converting leads into becoming clients.

These questions reveal things often referred to as pain points. Pain points are the specific problems that a current or prospective client may face on their journey. These problems can be recurring issues that regularly annoy, distress, or inconvenience your clients.

In most conversations with clients, the pain points are revealed easily. Many of them will tell you exactly what they're looking for and why. Then there are cases where getting a lead to reveal what they want is like pulling teeth. Knowing how to handle leads will increase the likelihood that the outcome will be what you and your client desire.

PURSUING THE PERFECT PROSPECT

Pain points are the hints to how we can solve a prospect's problem. The thing is, how does an agent find prospects to help? Again, most new agents will find their initial leads among friends and family, utilizing mutual connections to reach new people. While it's a common practice, it only gets an agent so far. Expanding on your client pool requires you to ask yourself some additional questions.

1. Where am I looking to sell?

2. Who am I looking to sell to?

These questions allow you to examine your own pain points. Taking an honest assessment of your pain points is the path that connects you with your target. When you start off by asking where you're looking to sell, you can start mapping out your plan. Location shows what issues and perks a prospect might encounter. Is the area prone to flooding? Is it near popular shopping areas? How are the schools in the area? What language is mostly spoken in the area? Once those are answered, you can use what you know about the location to investigate places where you can reach leads. Are their local coffee shops with community boards where you can leave a flyer? Are there country clubs where you can attend networking events and leave business cards? Are there places where you could advertise with a billboard? Answering where also applies to online efforts as you can utilize social media focused on specific locales to reach leads that are in the target area.

Determining who you are looking to sell to is an important step into establishing the identity of your leads. Are you looking to sell to first time homeowners that want to raise a family? Are you looking to sell to empty nesters looking to downsize? Making distinctions concerning who you're looking to sell to will make communicating with them easier. You wouldn't pitch a sale to the couple with a family of four in the same way you would a single person looking for a townhome. They have specific needs and concerns that aren't going to be satisfied in the same way. Identifying who you want to sell to lets agents become fluent in handling multiple lead types.

After those questions are answered, it's time to plan out how you are going to reach these prospective clients.

Lead generation requires consistency. Community events are a great way to connect with people in person. For example, let's say you're at a local fair and you get in line for a snack. There are people in that line that could potentially become a lead or refer you to a lead. The simplicity of making conversation can create the desired result. Other community events may allow you to have a booth or a table for a donation to an organization, such as a local library, that you can use to advertise what you offer as an agent. Social media is another way to generate leads in an affordable manner. By using your preferred platforms, you can use call to action features to create email lists. Emails are a great way to connect with and follow up with prospects outside of social media.

SPEAKING THEIR LANGUAGE

We've already established how communication or lack thereof could impact a prospect converting into a closed deal. The best way to learn how to speak to a prospect is to listen. It's a simple concept. Surprisingly, it's a skill that is often underutilized. When an agent is not actively listening, it can send a message to a prospect that they don't matter. That is the last message you want to send when attempting to close a deal. Just like in any conversation, the other party wants to know that they are heard, that they are seen as valued, and that they're being respected. When a prospect knows that they can check those boxes off with an agent, there may not be as many objections, or not as harsh if they do decline.

Taking the time to actively listen to a client helps to cut through the red tape. Being able to hear their concerns and convey a working solution shows the client that you are trustworthy and that they can have confidence that you are putting their interests above yours. Actively listening means that an agent is listening beyond the surface level of what the prospect is saying. They're listening for what is being said between the lines. Notetaking is a tool that helps with active listening as it makes it easier to get the details right, repeat them, and ask questions as necessary.

Empathy, concern, and compassion can go a long way in conversations with prospects. Usually, a knee-jerk reaction is to cut someone off when we have a possible solution or if we have an assumption of what they're going to say. Listening to them all the way through positions you to respond in a way that's human. Pitching to prospects can come across as cold and robotic if one is not careful. An agent should want to connect with a prospect's humanity. Why are they looking for a home in a particular neighborhood? Are they trying to lessen their commute to work? Do they want to be closer to family? Are they seeking the best education available for their children? These are the details that benefit buyer and agent as they qualify the prospect without being intrusive.

YouTube has videos with commonly heard rejections. Taking the time to familiarize yourself with rejections helps to respond to them in a way that doesn't feel like you're overriding the desires of the prospect. Sometimes the way agents handle rejections invalidates the legitimate concerns that a prospect has. Are they declining a space because they're not sure if the area is truly safe for them and their family? Are they rejecting a home because the value and the condition of it seem mismatched? Are they having second thoughts that purchasing a home is the right choice for them? Handling rejections and handling them well can quell the fears of a prospect and shift the odds in your favor.

Communication doesn't end when the deal closes. Follow-ups after a closed deal can open further doors. Let's say down the line the client wants to use you as an agent again. They already know that they can trust you because they have worked with you prior to, and follow-ups emphasize that you care. Follow-ups can also yield additional prospects. Clients that have good experiences working with an agent will not hesitate to tell other people about it. Following up gives you the room to ask if the client knows of anyone else that could benefit from working with you. Not only does the client see it as you care about them, but you also care about others that matter to them.

CURATING THEIR EXPERIENCE

The bottom line is that an agent should strive to use their customer service skills to give a prospect or a client the best possible experience. Strive to meet them where they are and remember that you don't have to adopt a fake persona to close a deal. Be authentic with them. Take all of the desires and concerns that they share with you and keep that in mind when you hold your open houses or take the prospects on a tour. You can show the prospect that you can create a world around their needs with what you show them.

Are they looking for granite countertops? How many bedrooms do they want? Is a pool something they would want? How big of a garage do they need? Once in a blue moon you might show a client a property that has everything that they're looking for at the price they want it at. In cases where they might not get everything they want; a client can still be satisfied if they could get almost everything or the things most essential to them.

When I did virtual tours on my social media, it allowed prospects to be there even if they weren't there physically. It created an experience that they could keep in the palm of their hands and re-experience at any time. When I held in-person open houses, I stopped to make sure that all who came in had a chance to feel like they were a priority. I've had people share their stories with me and then I went above and beyond to present them with a solution to their problem. Stellar customer service doesn't have to be complicated. At its core, treat the prospect the way that you would want to be treated in the same situation.

CHAPTER 4

Teamwork Makes The Dream Work

"Talent wins games, but teamwork and intelligence win championships."
—*Michael Jordan*

I started playing basketball in the sixth grade. It instilled a lot of character in me. When I was in the ninth grade, I became more intentional about my passion for the sport. The academics I was learning outside of class proved vigorous. I managed to finish the year with a 2.9 GPA, but I wasn't satisfied. There was a fire stirred up in me. I knew with every fiber of my being that my GPA could and should have been higher. I took the initiative to turn myself around by setting a goal to be excellent.

One of the most important values in basketball, or any sport for that matter, is the power of what you can accomplish as a team. There is a lot that one person can realize on their own. The principle of teamwork allows one to amplify what they can do. Teamwork should be effective and efficient. In order for that to happen, a new agent must be willing to find their tribe. One's tribe shouldn't be a group full of yes-men. A successful team has a variety of skills, viewpoints, and experiences that can achieve productive results across multiple scenarios. Building your team begins with a very specific step, and it's one that is often undervalued or overlooked.

TO KNOW THY TEAM, ONE MUST KNOW THYSELF

Teamwork requires the art of vulnerability. For many realtors starting out, a common misconception is that you have to go at it alone, especially in the beginning. "Rome wasn't built in a day," is a very common phrase that I'd like to make an addendum to. Rome wasn't built in a day, *and it wasn't built up alone.* Please don't think that you have to put yourself through undue stress by trying to take on everything by yourself at once. In the beginning, you think that you have to be your own marketing director, your own runner, your own social media team, etc. and that's not the case. In order to know who, I needed for my team, I looked inwards to determine what I needed help with.

Everyone's team will look different, and it will continue to evolve over time. What worked for me may not apply to you at present or at all. For me, an essential part of my team was my family. My parents taught me how to be resilient and how to fight for my goals, dreams, and what I wanted in life. Growing up in Baltimore, they faced and overcame a lot. They both are entrepreneurs and they worked hard so my siblings and I would want for nothing. Their entrepreneurial spirit and work ethic inspired me to pursue my own endeavors.

With the countless sacrifices my parents made, they never sacrificed the care of me and my siblings. The house was always clean. They were always present. My dad, Maurice, never allowed me to become arrogant. There are lessons that he taught me that stick with me to this very day. Those lessons have helped me to remain grounded and humble. My mom, Ericka, taught me about the risks of being an entrepreneur. There was a season where she encouraged me to pursue another job. However, I had knew the power of my own potential and I chose to bet on myself. No one in my family was making $100,000 from a corporate job straight out of college. The resilience my parents had was imparted in me and was the driving force behind me not settling. I watched them get up and go to work every day. I wouldn't have felt right if I didn't get up and pursue all that was in front of me.

The next person on my team was my mentor, Jason. I was a young, Black man starting in the industry. While many people of color often experience adversity in business, being a person of color provides a unique set of hurdles and frustrations to conquer. Jason taught me how to dress and how to articulate myself as a young, Black professional. My clients weren't all going to look, and sound like me. I had to develop the ability to have different conversations and know my audience well enough to articulate to them why I could add the most value to their journey of buying or selling a home. He broke down the essentials of everything that I needed to know.

Jason taught me a lot before I was even formally licensed. He encouraged me to join Keller Williams because they have one of the best training programs available, and it was a perfect supplement to the foundation he gave me. After I had a few sales underneath my belt, he encouraged me to join his company. But I liked where I was. I had gained an invaluable amount of knowledge there. The decision not to listen to my mentor ended up being costly to me as I didn't follow the opportunity that my mentor offered me. Despite the setback, Keller Williams was a big family to me, and I will forever appreciate my beginnings there.

My parents and mentor helped were the compasses that helped steer me at the start of my journey. Over time, I was exposed to more people and things that helped me better determine the type of team that I needed for my future. At the start of my real estate venture, I leaned on more on the frugal side because of what I was looking at financially at the time. Eventually I came to a point where I was able to hire out for the areas that I didn't have the time or energy to get to.

An agent isn't Superman. It's very easy to stretch yourself thin if you're not careful. When you're honest with yourself regarding your needs, you know what roles and tasks you can personally take on and which ones you need to hire out for. Some roles you may have to budget for and ultimately fold in after you've completed a substantial or considerate number of deals. Ultimately, the work you choose to do yourself should be the areas where you're most passionate about so your drive remains high even in the hard times.

WHO SHOULD I HIRE FOR MY TEAM?

Much like how some new agents feel they need to do all the work at once, there are other agents who feel as if they need to hire for every single role at one time. To reiterate, everyone's team will be different. There may be some roles that you need or don't need at all. I do believe that there are some areas that would be priorities to hire first. Some roles can be handled virtually to make things easier for an agent. For me, my time is extremely valuable. I was able to find a virtual assistant that is super helpful and fits my budget. Not only does hiring out roles allow me to get more done in a certain amount of time or budget, but it also allows me to be able to spend more time with my family or doing other things I want to do. Simply put, hiring out roles means that you can make your money work for you. Here are three areas that I believe you should look into hiring for as your capacity grows.

1. Administrative Assistant – As an agent, things run the risk of being all over the place. An administrative assistant is a great asset to keeping things in control. An administrative assistant can help with data entry tasks, managing your schedule, preparing documents, initiating and following up on correspondence, and making travel arrangements.

2. Transaction Coordinator – Transaction coordinators manage real estate transactions from start to finish. They gather information, documentation, and communication from all parties involved in the deal. They also can liaise with other real estate agents, inspectors, appraisers, and tradespeople on your behalf.

3. Social Media/Marketing Manager – Social media can be difficult for someone who isn't versed in

the business side of social media. Social media/ Marketing managers can create advertisements, set up marketing campaigns, create content that represents your brand voice, interpret online and offline marketing analytics. A social media/ marketing manager can also help with public relations as well by ensuring a constant presence for you on and offline.

Social Media is one of the areas where I for the time being handle it on my own. I like fresh and organic results. I like creating content that showcases my personal flair that doesn't come across as too generic or salesy. Sometimes there will be times when my sister will help me. She may prep a post as far as the design of it and then I handle the copy of the post. My sister's help eliminates me having to handle tasks that can eat up my time, leaving me freedom to handle the social media items that I want to focus on and ensuring that I can communicate the exact messaging I want.

CAN I USE SOFTWARE TO HELP MY TEAM?

The short answer is, yes! There are great software options out there that can make things easier for you and your team. There are options available to you even if you're not at an established level of funding or if you can't afford to have a more experienced person on your team, or if you just prefer to. One of my favorite tools is a customer relationship management tool, or CRM tool. This particular tool manages the interaction an agent has with their customers.

A CRM tool that I still use today is **Follow Up Boss.** Now I want to be clear that I'm not being endorsed by them. I want to share this program because it was taught to me when I was first starting out and it still helps me to this day. Follow Up Boss helps me track, organize, and communicate with my leads. When it comes to leads, you come into contact with multiple people and it's easy to lose track of vital information. With a CRM like Follow Up Boss, I can make sure contact with leads is consistent, I can see which leads are important, and most importantly, help me convert leads into sales.

For social media, you can look into tools such as **Hootsuite, Sprout Social**, and **Buffer.** These tools can help you schedule posts ahead of time, optimize your place in Google searches, publish popular articles, and reduce the time spent maintaining and increasing followers on your social media accounts. There are other helpful automation tools. **Google Workspace, Trello**, and **Todoist** work for administrative assistance and **Brokermint, Qualia,** and **Endpoint** are programs for transaction coordination. Wherever the need is, you can more than likely find a person or software that can handle the needs of you and your team.

WHAT A TEAM MEANS TO ME

My team reflects on me and my business. I don't discriminate in showing support for the people that are on my team. Respect goes from the leader and all the way down to the assistants. I view them as extensions of myself because we typically ride the same wavelength as far as standards or ethics. I wouldn't feel comfortable recommending someone that would give a client a negative experience because that in turn can backfire on me. Unfortunately, I've had that happen. I once made the mistake of referring a photographer to a client that wasn't a good fit for their needs. The photographer didn't hold the same standard of excellence that I expected, and they missed the mark. As a result, I had to send a second photographer to complete the job that the first one couldn't.

My team is my tribe. They work with me on the front lines. They are the people I look up to. They are where I am and where I want to be. They add value to my life and my career. They encourage me, motivate me, and guide me. That's how it should be for any agent looking to build their team. The best part about having a team or tribe is that I don't have to reinvent the wheel. If I happen to be going through a difficult situation or time, I don't have to figure things out by myself. They are a safety net of support that I can call and get advice from. They can help me avoid mistakes and see opportunities that I might have missed. Create the tribe that you want to see and the tribe that you believe you deserve. You have to believe in the team you create, because at the end of the day, the team you believe in reflects the you that you believe in. Believe in your team of you and believe in your team. Then watch how far you can go.

CHAPTER 5
Take Time For You

"It's important to have a balance in your life between work and play."
—*Bobby Flay*

Has there ever been a point in your life where you feel as though time is slipping past you? You find yourself hunched over your desk scrawling over report after report. You're checking if your finances are in the black or in danger of going in the red. There's so much heavily weighing on your mind. Burnout lies in wait to drag you down like a rip current. There's so much to do and little time to do it. Meanwhile, life goes on, and you feel like if you're not careful it will slip away before you can grasp it.

We live in a world where hustle culture is the norm. Social media teaches us to strive for lifestyles that may not be meant for us. Yet we want it because the grass looks greener compared to what we have. You hear things like, "Team no sleep" or "I'll sleep when I'm dead." We don't have a concept of rest. We're like the Energizer battery. We keep going and going and going until we can't go anymore. In the moment, it seems like that approach will yield a lot. However, we find that it's a style and mindset that robs us blind.

We miss important milestones. We sacrifice birthdays and anniversaries. We're present in body, but not in the moment we're needed. Then what happens is that life takes a moment to slap us in the face, bringing us back into the present. We realize what we have before us is slowly wasting away because there are areas of our lives that we're neglecting for the sake of success. It is often said that if we don't take care of ourselves that we can't take care of others or the things that we need to. So we have to take the time to stop and consider the cost. *Is success worth losing ourselves in the process?*

The average person may say yes because they want something better than what they have. They want cars, money, a house with the white picket fence and a dog, etc. But in the end, those desires only treat the symptoms of where we're empty. Those desires don't fill us the way we need to be filled. We create personas based on things that are temporary and/or untrue. It's baffling that some are willing to give up a truly awesome life for things that may not even give them fulfillment in life.

Before we go any further, I want you to think about where you're at in life. I want you to think about the things that you have experienced. Think about the things that you have given up to get to the place where you want to be. Now I want you to take a moment to be honest with yourself; is where you are now the place that you *really* want to be? Do you feel like your life is going in a direction that is authentic to you and your journey? Are you striving towards the place that you want to see yourself in the next five to ten years? I know that you may struggle with wanting to answer those questions. But you need to answer them before you risk losing it all.

MISTAKES CAN MAKE YOU OR BREAK YOU

I'm just as human as all of you who are reading this book. From time to time, I've made mistakes that I've had no choice but to grow from. Some of them I thought would be the end of my world as I knew it. I had to learn how to press and push through. There were days where I wanted to give up. There were days I didn't know who I was. There were days where I felt so lost. All I wanted to do was become the person I knew that I always was. But there was a time where I had started to become someone so contrary to who I am. I felt like a stranger in my own body.

In December 2020, I hung my license. For those just entering this field, hanging or parking your license refers to the broker that supervises you and your activities. There are particular responsibilities that come with being a supervising broker. They check the quality of your work and they make sure you're performing to a standard that's ethical. In a way, you can say that you hanging your license not only reflects you, but the brokerage that you're a part of.

It was around this time where I had already gained some knowledge about real estate. I was working a corporate job that paid me pretty handsomely. It was my dream job. I bought a Range Rover. I got accustomed to living a certain lifestyle. I obtained my dream job at the age of 21. I didn't realize how this job was already seeping its way into my identity. It was something that started to define me. Here I was taking on this new venture in real estate on top of my job, and everything looked pretty sweet. But I couldn't have been more wrong.

Two and a half months later, I was fired. Everything I had built up to that point now was crumbling beneath me. My world was falling apart because the rug had now been pulled from beneath my feet. I ended up having an identity crisis. It took a bit of time to recenter myself in order to find who I was. I wasn't going to risk losing myself and losing sight of my dream again.

I also made the mistake of not setting boundaries between my work and personal life. There have been times where I have gone out to dinner with friends and my phone would ring incessantly. Each and every time, I found myself answering the calls. This was business and I hoped my friends would understand. Nevertheless, I knew in my heart that it only annoyed them. In my mind I was only taking care of business, and I had to do what I had to do. I couldn't see how rude it was. I couldn't see that I wasn't truly present with those that loved and cared for me. I was robbing them of time with me and I was robbing myself of being able to properly value the people that were placed in my life.

I had to get everything together or else I ran the risk of losing everything that mattered to me. I couldn't give up. I had to learn from my mistakes and start anew. It was a process that pruned me for the better and the reason why I have the accolades that I do. Mistakes made me a better businessman and a better *man*. What saddens me is that is not the reality for other people, and they are left broken by their past. I don't want that to be you. That is why I am proud of you for picking up this book and for letting me walk alongside you on your journey.

TO THINE OWN SELF BE TRUE

I had to learn to take the time to take care of me totally and fully. Many would think that self-care is selfish.

It's not. As a matter of fact, it's necessary. Self-care is a deliberate act of preservation. If you don't take the time to manage you, you leave yourself open to things like being taken advantage of, mental and emotional frustration, and the pain of feeling like all of your hard work is going to be wasted and your life is going nowhere.

I needed to be intentional about taking the time to recharge. Sometimes that looks like me getting a massage or going out to enjoy an event. At times it's me literally unplugging and putting my phone on Do Not Disturb so I can spend time with friends and family without being distracted. I remember my dad and sister coming to help me during a recent move. As they were helping me get things set up, I had unintentionally left my phone in my room as we worked. It was the best happy accident that could have happened. I was able to be present and enjoy that time with my family. Whether it's for fifteen minutes, thirty minutes, or an hour, unplug. Take that time and invest it in something you enjoy. Invest it in bettering yourself. Invest in giving yourself the rest that you need. Do not deny yourself rest because you need it. There are things you rob yourself of if you don't get the proper rest mentally, physically, and emotionally. Invest your time wisely and enjoy the fruits of it.

RECALIBRATING THE VISION

As an agent, you have to believe in yourself. You have to believe in what you do, and you have to stand ten toes down when things don't go the way they plan. You have to be wholeheartedly dedicated to your mission. Make space in your schedule to create a plan. Map out the steps that lead to your goals being realized. I feel as though there are many people out there that have these big dreams and visions. But they don't have a plan to get there. Having visions of grandeur doesn't automatically mean you're going to achieve those things. You have to do the work necessary to bring the harvest of your hands into fruition.

Let's say that you have a goal to sell 35 homes in a year. The question is, how? How are you going to gain the target goal of clients and how are you going to sell these homes to them? What is your strategy? Does that look like hosting open houses? Are you seeking referrals from past clients and peers in the field. Are you making cold calls and knocking on doors? How are you going to get from point A, to B, and ideally, to Z?

My goal for 2021 was to sell at least 20 houses. I took the time to write the vision and make it plain so the way to achieve that goal was always on the top of my mind. My strategy required that I have three avenues or pillars that I wanted to pursue in order to obtain those clients. I made sure the instructions were clear so I didn't overwhelm myself in the process and to ensure that the actual plan made sense.

The first step was hosting two open houses a week. I wanted to know names and faces. I wanted to see who I was potentially going to connect to. I wanted people to establish rapport with me so they could trust me with their business. I had a goal in mind to gain five to seven new clients from the open houses. Step two was executing my social media strategy. I marketed myself on various platforms. I did virtual tours and created graphics to catch people's attention. I used social media as a way to show leads that I was accessible for their needs. I set an objective of obtaining ten clients from social media marketing. The third and final step was cold-calling properties that were listed as either for sale by the owner or where the listing had expired. This put me directly on the path of reaching the right people. The criteria for this step was that I acquired 3 new clients from. Being in real estate requires you to have three to four pillars to support your business and help you realize your unit goal.

I also had to take a step back and take inventory of where I was getting in my own way and where I was thriving. One of my problem areas was having the trust and expectations that others would handle things in the way and standard that I would. In hindsight, that wasn't a realistic expectation because everyone works in the way that works best for them. This ended up causing me to micromanage my team at times because I desired perfection and needed to be sure that things were done to the level of excellence I wanted to see.

On the opposite end, one of my strengths was being a great leader. Hold on, I know you're saying, *Montaz, just a moment ago you were micromanaging people. How could you be a micromanager AND a good leader?* Well, I'll tell you. What made me a good leader was that I was not afraid to get in the field and get my hands dirty. My team is small. It's only my admin, my executive assistant, and myself. I strove to be as genuine as possible with them. I wasn't going to tell someone to do something that I hadn't done or that I didn't believe would add value to the group as a whole. I sought to do things in the spirit of generosity. I wanted all who worked with me to be on a team where everything was mutually beneficial for all. I wanted to win and I wanted my team to win too. So I did what I could to make sure that happened.

PEACE BY ANY MEANS NECESSARY

Honestly speaking, real estate is extremely time consuming and demanding. It can encapsulate your entire life. I implore you to spend time with your family. Go do something you love or something that you've always wanted to do. I know what it's like to be glued to your phone because you don't want to miss an opportunity. I'm begging you, turn the phone off for a little bit. I'm going to be real with you and share with you an affirmation that has been key to my life; *What is for me will always find a way to me.*

Some days I couldn't get a good workout in. There were times where I didn't leave my house without my laptop. I had moments where I couldn't enjoy being with my friends or family, and it was all because I wanted to be available to take a call or cater to the needs of my client. I learned that most things could wait, most notably if it's after hours. Clients that cannot respect your boundaries or your time more than likely aren't your ideal client.

Everyone deserves to have a break and spend time with their loved ones. Everyone deserves to have time to go on vacation or spend some time relaxing and just being in the moment. I've made every effort to spend time and cherish every moment with those I love dearly because that is time that I will never get back. Weigh the cost of what you desire and pursue it in a way that is realistic to you so that life doesn't pass you by in the blink of an eye.

CHAPTER 6
Believe In Yourself

"Trust yourself. Create the kind of self that you will be happy to live with all your life. Make the most of yourself by fanning the tiny, inner sparks of possibility into flames of achievement."
—*Golda Meir*

Have you ever had times in your life where you were on the verge of something? Maybe it was something tangible, like accomplishing a goal. Or maybe, it was a bit more abstract, like feeling yourself mature. Did you ever feel scared in those moments? Did you ever feel as though you couldn't do what you believed you were being led to do? You may have felt a form of imposter syndrome. Imposter syndrome is cruel. It's anxiety about something you already know how to do, but you believe that you are unable to do it because you now have to do it at a level that you've never done before.

Motivational speaker Les Brown once said, "The graveyard is the richest place on earth, because it is here that you will find all the hopes and dreams that were never fulfilled, the books that were never written, the songs that were never sung, the inventions that were never shared, the cures that were never discovered, all because someone was too afraid to take that first step, keep with the problem, or determined to carry out their dream." Graves full of unrealized and untapped potential. Purpose and hope forced to prematurely rot and waste.

No one wants to live life unfulfilled. The reality is, we're all at risk of doing that when we let fear take a hold of the steering wheel of our lives. There's a well-known acronym about fear. Fear is *False Evidence Appearing Real*. Realistically speaking, we know that if we try something new there is a chance that we might fail. We also have an equal chance of success. Fear, makes you paint what's in front of you with a broad brush. You may have done something a million times over with no issue and fear will make you believe that this is the one time where you will mess up. Regardless of what it is you do in life, do not let fear rob you of living life to your fullest potential.

FACE YOUR FEARS

Often, fear creeps in when we don't have a true understanding of our inner potential. When we are ignorant of that, the challenges that we face in a situation then appear as though they outnumber us. We start talking about all the things that we *think* we can't do as if they are things we legitimately cannot do. We come up with excuses and rationalize the reasons why we refuse to try. The most fatal mistake of it all is that we end up treating failure as final. Failure is only final if you refuse to learn from it and keep moving.

We've already established earlier that there are a lot of risks to real estate. Anything in your life that you find worth doing will have risks. But more often than not, those risks yield big rewards. You might go back into the previous chapters and see some of the things you have to do and be like, *Man, Montaz. I don't know if I'm cut out for this.* How are you going to know if you don't try? How are you going to try with a defeatist attitude? Stop the negative self-talk. If you didn't have the potential to do it, the drive that got you started wouldn't have been there.

I previously mentioned that I had a corporate job before I started real estate. I did well at my corporate job. When I added real estate into the mix, I was beyond ecstatic that I was going to have two lucrative careers. But because I was so ambitious to make both work, I didn't realize that I was starting to slack up at my corporate job. So not only was I fired due to lack of performance, I was also fired because they found out about my real estate endeavors.

Losing my job was an incredibly shocking blow. It was a horrible feeling to know that I lost a job that paid me nearly six figures and all the hard work I did in college to get to that job was now down the drain. My mom encouraged me to find another position. As much as she cheered me on, she was very wary of me pursuing a career in real estate. In fact, she advised that I should move forward from real estate all together. Her concerns were valid. The pay scale in real estate can be ambiguous. However, what made things so much more difficult for me was that I began my real estate career in the middle of the COVID-19 pandemic. There were just too many concerns for her to have full confidence in my real estate career.

I was in the middle of the unknown. I didn't know how things were going to work out or if they even would work out. Others in my life voiced their concerns as well. Realizing that I didn't have the support from those I loved and cared about was hard. When you're going through times of uncertainty, you want to be able to go to the people around you and let them be your emotional safety net. But what do you do when that net is gone?

I had no choice but to become my own cheerleader. I pressed forward to begin building my real estate career. The first five months of it were long and hard. I wasn't selling any houses. It seemed like everything was slipping through my fingers. I chose to grasp what I could and make the most of what I had in my hands. I sought out the wisdom that I would need in order to make this career work, and for me to learn how to survive while doing it.

I soaked up as much knowledge as possible. I went to experienced agents and asked questions. I helped out other agents by showing houses on their behalf. I watched webinar after webinar. I learned whatever I had to because the future I saw for myself demanded that I become my best self in order to achieve it. This might be the most controversial thing that you will ever hear me say in this book, but it has to be said. *You cannot maximize mediocre.*

NO HALF STEPPING

I know that we live in a day and age where many individuals attempt to manifest their desires with their thoughts. Thinking in an elevated manner is helpful, but you have to do the work necessary in order to grow. If you go to the gym because you want abs, you can't think your way through having them. You have to put in the time and energy to work out. You have to discipline your eating. You have to get the proper amount of sleep. I could go on and on. Thinking about your goals is a great way to start, but you can't just leave things in the hands of your thoughts. You have to put in the work.

You cannot use shortcuts or skip steps when it comes to obtaining the life that you want. If you skipped steps in baking a cake, the cake would turn out crummy. *No pun intended.* You wouldn't be able to enjoy the cake as it was meant to be intended because some necessary ingredients were missing. If I didn't tough out those five months, I would not be writing this book for you today. If I didn't endure all the blood, sweat, and tears to rebuild my life after losing my job then I would have lost everything else.

I had to connect with the me that I always knew was there. I had to be honest with myself about the things that scared me about this part of my journey. I had to show up for myself every day because not that many people were willing to show up for me. I know that it is upsetting not having certain people by your side when you want them to be there. It's okay to feel those things.

You have to know that there will be seasons on your journey that require you to move alone or with a smaller, specific party. I understand that you might want to bring others along with you. However, not everyone is meant to go into the same spaces that you are called to go. Sometimes we have to go into these seasons alone because there is something specifically for us by the other side of it.

After all the time I spent pushing myself, everything ended up working out in the end. All of the hard work had paid off and then some. I learned that just because some people love you and have good intentions towards you, does not mean that their opinion is an absolute law. I know that my mom had my best interests at heart. She was simply trying to protect me, not just as my mom, but as my peer in entrepreneurship. She wanted me to be safe.

Still, some of the visions and dreams that we have will not make sense to other people. The fight for our future cannot be contingent on whether or not others get or agree with what we're going to do. It's still okay to listen to people when they give advice as they might see vantage points that you don't. However, take the meat of what they say and spit out the bones of what isn't necessary.

DREAM BIG

Before we go into the next chapter, I want you to stop for a moment. I want you to think about all the things that you wanted to do but never did because you were scared. I want you to write them down and then I want you to write down the exact fear that kept you from doing it. The reason why I want you to do this is because I want you to get familiar with your pattern of thinking and how it syncs in with what you feel. Do you see the same fears popping up? When those fears come up, how do you respond to them? Do you give up? Do you get emotional? Now we're going to take this and use it as fuel.

Next, I want you to think about your real estate goals. I want you to think about what it is that you want to accomplish. Now I want you to think about the things that could potentially stop you from achieving it. As you write those things down, I want you to compare the fears you have pertaining to real estate with the fears that you had about the stuff you didn't accomplish. Do you see any similarities? Do you notice any differences?

Once you have identified your concerns and your past fears, I want you to make a promise to yourself that even if things scare you that you won't run away or back down. Use those fears as soil to grow and get better in. Do it afraid and do it anyway. There is a version of you on the other side of this battle. This version of you comes from the fruit of you putting in your heart, soul, and effort into. Is that person worth becoming? Do you deserve to become that person that you see? I hope you answered yes.

If you hesitate to answer those questions, you're going to find yourself stuck in life. Don't let your dreams go with you to the grave. Go boldly and live them out. If you really feel as though you cannot do something you're presented with, then go do what you need to in order to become confident in those areas. You deserve what is on the other side of this. Even if others don't believe in you, the party of one can more than make up for it when it has to. At the end of the day, God put the promise in *you*! You are the only one who is going to see the vividness of your vision. Don't lose heart if other people do not see what you see. They will see it if and when they are meant to. Take a step out in faith and see the vision through. Face your fears until your fears fear you. I promise you that it will all be worth it.

CHAPTER 7

Success Through Scriptures

"But remember the LORD your God, for it is He who gives you the ability to produce wealth, and so confirms His covenant, which He swore to your ancestors, as it is today."

—*Deuteronomy 8:18*

There comes a point in our lives where we realize how much bigger our lives are. I know there are people out there who think about where they were five or ten years ago and see how much their views about themselves have changed. I know there are people out there who never could have imagined one day wanting to find a way to change the world with what they do.

Ahem, Montaz. This is a book about real estate. You can't change the world with that. It's not that deep.

Au contraire, my friend. You can change the world through real estate, and yes, it is that deep.

You see, real estate revealed that in the grand scheme of things, my God-given purpose was to impact the lives of other people. There are many people in the world who dream of having a home, and fear that they may never get to own one. There are people who desire to find housing where they can live comfortably and not worry about if they will have to physically struggle to get out of the house. There are parents out there who want to ensure that their child will be around things that will help them flourish in life. It's more than houses, y'all.

Seeing what my earning potential could be in real estate inspired me to move in this direction. In all honesty, I want to work in a way that allows me to retire at thirty. I know that may seem outlandish to some. I know that for some out there, life begins at thirty and there's no harm in that. But I don't want to do real estate for the rest of my life. Real estate is the soil that my calling needs to grow. It's more than houses, y'all.

In the dreams that I have for me beyond real estate, I want to start a non-profit or a foundation. I want to be a blessing to other people. This book is a part of that desire. I get to share the knowledge that I have gained with you and others reading this, so you don't have to go through the painful things I went through just to get it. This book is even able to help some of you prepare for the painful parts of this journey that you won't be able to avoid. There will be courses that come from this in the future. There are mentees out there that I have yet to meet. Say it with me this time; *it's more than houses, y'all.*

I believe that there are things in this life that God wants to give us. I believe that when we walk in our calling, favor follows us and acts as a magnet. Favor will attract blessings that you never saw coming. You'll attract some haters too. However, the point of them is to remind you just how blessed you are. What's amazing about having a God-given purpose is that His word is full of wisdom that can help us on our journeys of fulfilling them. There are some stories and scriptures that I believe serve as eagle eyes in business.

THINKING OF A MASTER PLAN

Habakkuk 2:2-3 – "Then the LORD replied: "Write down the revelation and make it plain on tablets so that a herald may run with it. For the revelation awaits an appointed time; it speaks of the end and will not prove false. Though it linger, wait for it; it will certainly come and not delay."

This verse is so powerful because it speaks to how we are to approach the visions that God gives us. Remember in chapter one how I asked you what your dreams and goals were? When we start casting vision, we're bringing those dreams to the forefront. We're moving them from being thoughts and establishing a plan to manifest them. You may not have all the steps written out and there may be some challenges that you won't know of until you face them. But beginning the process of writing them down allows you to prepare and plan as much as possible. You begin to figure out what you might need and can eliminate what you don't need down the line.

Now this verse also speaks to what we addressed in chapter four. When you write down your vision and develop a business plan from it, you are then able to effectively communicate what you see with the people that are on your team. They won't have to do guesswork as to how they can help you because either:

1. You'll assign them somewhere specific need based on your vision.

2. They will tell you how their particular gifts and talents can fill your needs and then run to execute the part of your vision that they are responsible for.

Lastly, this verse brings home one of the points I've emphasized throughout the book so far, trusting the process. If a farmer plants a seed in the ground, the harvest doesn't come up as soon as they plant it. The seed has to be buried deep in the ground and they won't be able to see it sprout for some time as most of the growth will be underground and out of sight. But the farmer doesn't worry because they know that the harvest is coming in due season. As you go through this journey of being a realtor, remember that your efforts are a seed. You're not going to see overnight success. There will be times when things will look as if nothing is happening. Still, press onward and wait for that vision to come to pass because it will.

I'M CALLED FOR THIS

Ephesians 2:10 - "For we are God's handiwork, created in Christ Jesus to do good works, which God prepared in advance for us to do."

I've shared some stories about the early part of my journey. Remember, I got discouraged a lot. One of the things that you're going to have to remember in the process is that God will place you where you need to be. He will give you the skills to do the work that you need to do. Some skills you will naturally have. Others will be acquired when you go out in the field or learn from other people in the industry. God will never call you to something and then not prepare you for what He asked you to do. I know it's scary feeling like you don't know what you're doing. When that feeling rises up, let God surprise you by bringing out what He knew was in you all along.

SOWING SEEDS

Proverbs 21:5 - "The plans of the diligent lead surely to abundance, but everyone who is hasty comes only to poverty."

Consistency is key *and* king. This may seem redundant for a second but bear with me. Let's go back to that illustration that I gave you of the farmer. Now, the farmer might use things like fertilizer to help in the process of growing his harvest. Some things will help speed up the process and others will help the harvest to grow healthy. A seasoned farmer is going to be wise about what he uses and what he exposes those seeds to. If he's not, then he runs the risk of destroying the harvest and all of his hard work going to waste.

Do not treat real estate as if it's some get rich quick thing. If you do, then you will find yourself wasting money and time. Real estate is serious. You can't take shortcuts in it. There are laws that you're going to have to be aware of. You have to conduct yourself in a manner that allows you to attract and retain clients and team members. If you don't have the right mindset going into it, you will find yourself ready to quit as soon as you start, wallowing in a pit of bad information, or both.

Take the time to do things right. Remain levelheaded in all you do. Then, you will be able to healthily handle success when it comes. And yes, you need to have character that will sustain you after the sales start coming in. That's what will allow you to be flexible to learn new things and stay humble. Acting as though you know everything will only get you so far. Take your time, be smart with it, and be consistent.

ELEVATING ABOVE THE HATERS AND NAYSAYERS

Colossians 3:23 - "Whatever you do, work heartily, as for the Lord and not for men, knowing that from the Lord you will receive the inheritance as your reward. You are serving the Lord Christ."

Nehemiah 6:9 - "For they all wanted to frighten us, thinking, 'Their hands will drop from the work, and it will not be done.' But now, O God, strengthen my hands.'"

These verses are for the times where you encounter haters or have to deal with the loved ones who don't get it. As we are walking in our God-given purpose, there will be moments where God will shut the eyes of other people so they can't see what He's doing in your life. That may seem counterintuitive, but God does it to protect the vision He gave you. Unfortunately, there are people in this world who are dream killers. Some of them don't mean to do it. Then there are those who deliberately go out of their way to do it. Anything that God does has to come to completion, and there are things seen and unseen that want to try to get in the way of that.

If the dream in you can't be killed, then the next thing that comes is distraction. Distractions cause you to waste time, energy, and resources. Make sure that you are rooted when you start moving in your purpose. Do not look to the right or the left. Keep your eyes on the prize. I know it sounds cliché, but vision requires focus. If you don't focus then what happens is that blessings become burdens. You run the risk of losing heart for what God called you to do.

Also, it is important to do this unto God because it helps anchor you to your why. I was honest with you at the start of this chapter; I want to be able to retire from real estate by the age of thirty so I can focus on helping people in the other ways that God calls me to. That is part of my why. So when things get hard, I can remember that God called me to do it and why He picked me. The same goes for you. God could have picked another, but He picked you because there is a uniqueness to you that the world needs in the areas you're assigned. Do not lose sight of that. Once again, it's more than houses, y'all.

SAVE SOME GRACE FOR YOU

Psalm 127:2 - "It is in vain that you rise up early and go late to rest, eating the bread of anxious toil; for he gives to his beloved sleep."

Remember how we talked about self-care in chapter five? Rest is important, so take it when you have to. If you don't take the time to rest then all that you do is going to be in vain and you won't enjoy it. I also want to use this verse to highlight not operating in a state of anxiety. If you go into this and experience seasons where things aren't working, do not continue operating as if the floor is going to cave beneath you going forward. Setbacks are seasonal, not permanent.

Lastly, I want you to read the story of Joseph when you have the chance. His story shows everything that we've discussed in this chapter. In addition to that, his story also shows how the ways in which we do business can affect other people. Joseph was not only able to save his family, but he was also able to save an entire nation. The things we do may not be as grand as what he did. That should not deter us as there will be those that we encounter in our careers that will never hear the story of Joseph or pick up a Bible, but they will know *our* story. They will see what happens in our lives and be reminded that living the life you want to live is possible. It's more than just houses, y'all. Trust God and all that He is doing in and through you. Let Him blow your mind. Once He does, you'll never be the same again.

CHAPTER 8

Systems Make Things Easier

"Systems and processes are essential to keep the crusade going, but they should not replace the crusade."

—*Simon Sinek*

In our current day and age, our minds are going a million miles a minute trying to keep up with the hustle and bustle of the world around us. There is a constant push to be able to multitask. As we are people and not octopi, we can only stretch ourselves so far. When building your business, you want to be able to work efficiently and in excellence. Ideally, you should create systems that can help you to do such.

The way that I'm building my business is so I can replace myself having to be in certain areas with someone else down the line. In all honesty, we cannot be everything to everyone. As we addressed in chapter four, I know I can conquer way more with a team than on my own. The best solo agents have teams of admins and assistants that help support their business constantly.

Communication and clarity are vital. By building out a system, you create a path of success for anyone that will follow in your footsteps.

I know, I know. I hear those wheels turning in your head.

Montaz, where do I even begin to build a system? I don't even know what one looks like.

Aht. Aht. You're already making it more complicated than what it is. Plus, if you've read this far, do you really think I'm going to leave you hanging? Don't worry, I got you.

MAKING THE VISION PLAIN PART 1

In the last chapter we talked about the principles of Habakkuk 2:2-3 and how it's the perfect basis for creating a business plan. I would like to emphasize once again, putting your thoughts to paper is the first step in creating a business plan. You want to make sure the ideas that you have in your head are cohesive enough once you verbalize them aloud or write them down. If they're not, then you have to start considering where to tweak the idea in order for it to make sense. Creating a business plan may seem daunting at first. But once you answer these six simple questions, you'll have an easier time formulating the plan. These six main questions can help you expand on your ideas with essential sub-questions that can help you cement your ideas. Those six questions are:

a. Who?
- Who do I want to sell to/buy from?
- Who do I want/need on my team?
- Who can I learn from/connect with?

b. What?
- What do I need to do to generate leads?
- What do I need to do to form my team?
- What do I need to do to improve my skills?
- What licenses do I need to have?
- What paperwork do I need to fill out?
- What do I need to give my clients/leads excellent service?
- What does my team need in order to be successful?
- What do I need to do should I have to pivot?

c. Where?
- Where am I looking to sell?
- Where do I need to go to network?
- Where can I market myself on/offline?
- Where do I see my business in the next 5/10/20 years?

d. When?
- When do I want to accomplish my goals by?

- When do I need to follow up with leads/ clients by?
- When do I need to hold progress meetings with my team?
- When do I need to recertify important licensure?
- When should I review the direction that my business is going?

e. How?
  - How do I want to brand myself?
  - How do I want to communicate with my team?
  - How do I want to engage with leads/clients?
  - How do I set myself apart from competitors in the area?
  - How do I improve my business?
  - How often should I review the direction of my business?

f. Why?
  - Why do I want to work in this particular area?
  - Why do I need to follow up with particular clients?
  - Why am I motivated to do things in this particular way?
  - Why do I want these specific people on my team?

MAKING THE VISION PLAIN PART 2

Now that you have answered those six questions and the follow-up questions, it's time to start writing the business plan. The business plan is the most important document that you will ever write. It's more important than a logo or pushing your brand because you will have neither of those things without an established business plan. Business plans will help you prepare for the worst and ensure that you can enjoy the best. According to the National Association of Realtors, there are seven elements to developing a solid business plan. Those elements are:

a. Mission Statement – This is where you illustrate the motivation and core of your business. It should be easy to understand and thoroughly explain the advantages of working with you.

b. SWOT Assessment - SWOT stands for strengths, weaknesses, opportunities, and threats. This analysis requires you to reflect on yourself as a realtor and the environment that you're working in accordance with the SWOT acronym.

c. Specific Goals – Determine your goals and identify which are short-term goals and which are long-term goals. Your short-term goals should sustain the long-term goals that you have.

d. Strategic Plan – Identify how you plan to reach your goals. This plan will change over time as your business, team, and abilities develop.

e. Time Frame – Schedule deadlines for all of your goals in order to guarantee that you will remain dedicated and responsible as those goals come to completion.

f. Target Audience – Pinpoint your ideal clientele and market to adjust your plan as needed.

g. Systems and Processes – Develop the necessary systems and processes to attain success.

SETTING UP YOUR SYSTEM

The last thing I want to go over with you in this chapter is how to set up the systems that you are going to use. I created a very simple acronym to help you remember the steps. Though it may sound silly, it is an effective way to bring your systems to life. I want you to SERVE COALS and this is what it looks like:

a. Survey - Create a checklist of your business movements for a period of time (1 week min. - 1 month max)

b. Establish - Review the list for time consuming and recurring tasks

c. Record - Write down all of the necessary steps to satisfy the previously identified tasks.

d. Verify - Determine what parts of each step can be streamlined.

e. Explore - Research tools and software to assist in streamlining the work.

f. Combine - Incorporate the tools you found and utilize them in accomplishing the tasks.

g. Organize - Create detailed guides for each component. Include graphics, charts, templates, and written/visual demonstrations as needed.

h. Assign - Determine who on your team will take on each part of the process.

i. Level Up - Listen for feedback from your team to address issues as they arise and improve productivity.

j. Strike While The Iron's Hot - Take advantage of the new openings in your schedule to handle the tasks that you want/need to give attention to.

Taking the steps above is a surefire way to create a plan that is conducive to your business. It may seem arduous to follow all these steps, but you have to remember that *anything worth building is worth building correctly.* If you rush the process, you're bound to have cracks in your foundation. Allow the systems you create to work things out for you and see just how much you can accomplish when everything flows as it should.

CHAPTER 9

Building From The Ground Up

"Starting a business is like jumping out of an airplane without a parachute. In mid air, the entrepreneur begins building a parachute and hopes it opens before hitting the ground."
—*Robert Kiyosaki*

Pause for a moment. You have come a long way. You've had this vision about real estate burning in your heart for some time. Now you are at a point where you are on the cusp of bringing your vision to reality. In comparison with the preparations, executing the vision is often the hardest part.

This is the moment where you begin to see how much pressure you can take. Will you break the moment that your knees begin to buckle, or will you bend? Do you go to sleep dreaming about how close you are to having all that you want in your hands? I'm not limiting that to just money, I want to know how on fire you are for everything that you want to accomplish.

Not everyone has what it takes to go into real estate. This entrepreneurial life can be extremely demanding. On one hand there's going to be a lot of frustration when things first start. On the other, there is a great joy knowing that all you have worked towards is unfolding before your very eyes. I want you to be proud of yourself for making it this far. I will be even prouder knowing that you are well on your way to achieving your dreams.

I see you laying out every single brick. You have the mortar ready to hold the whole thing in place. You have the blueprints in your hands. It's time to start building. I know you feel the tightness in your chest. There's an excitement that has just a tinge of doubt in the corner. You put your hands forward, picking up the first tool you have, and you begin.

You're scared.

I know, I've been there too. But remember, you got this.

I want you to build as high as your dream will take you.

A FIRM FOUNDATION

Failure and patience go hand in hand. Building a deep foundation as a realtor means you have to be realistic about certain things. Success doesn't come overnight in most cases. You don't automatically become wealthy with your very first sale or on a really big one. You have to learn how to build a big business. Then you have to go and build it.

You can go to a brokerage that gives you 100% of your commissions, but that still may not be the best place for you if they are not teaching you the essentials of building a real estate business. Do you know how generate leads? Do you know how to work your sphere? Do they provide open house opportunities? Is there someone to mentor you and help foster your growth? Do you know how to get business? If you don't know how to do that, then there's no commission to earn. You have to go somewhere that will teach you the ropes. You might get frustrated that things are off to a slow start. You will probably have a few transactions under your belt before you really begin to see how the work is paying off.

Go and build yourself a foundation that supports you as you build on it. Don't skip steps. Don't disparage the dirty work. That only hinders your growth. I wanted to be able to give my team instructions. Sometimes I would go into the office of a more experienced agent and go over things like home inspection reports, so I knew what I was doing. This was how I learned to add value to everything that I did and add value to my clients' experience.

There were days where I was discouraged and wanted to give up. There were days where I was intimidated by some of the expenses that I had to pay while I was trying to build my portfolio as a realtor. I had to figure out how to make things work. I had to fight through days that just depressed me. I had to make my own sacrifices. I had to make myself get up early and show up for myself. Building a foundation isn't easy, but if it's not done properly, everything else will fall apart.

I had to put myself in a mindset that forced me to build upwards. I had to come up in my thinking because if I didn't, I would only build something that was low and safe. I didn't want that for my legacy. I wanted to build as high as my limits could go and then break past them. The next level was in my reach, I just had to mentally go there.

I kept a target in my mind with the fish that I wanted to catch. I knew the potential clientele I wanted, and I did everything I could to capture them. I learned to walk the walk and talk the talk. They understood me. They saw why I was worth trusting with their business. It took time for things to come through. But when they did, I was reminded that everything was worth it.

MENTOR MENTALITY

The best thing about being in the realm of real estate is that I didn't have to reinvent the wheel. Others were already in this business for a long time, so I didn't have to do everything on my own. Back in chapter four, I mentioned that I had multiple mentors. I looked to my parents and all they did for our family. I connected with my mentor Jason, who gave me a map for success. I was hungry to learn and even hungrier for my dream.

Because of the various mentors that I had in my career, I wanted to honor the work that they did with and in me. I was able to mentor other people through this book.

See, to be a great mentor, you have to be a great student. You have to be willing to listen and learn. You cannot be afraid to ask questions. You cannot be afraid to get things wrong while you're still getting things sorted out in the beginning. Develop an insatiable appetite for knowledge and it will preserve you, your business, and all of those who are attached to it.

Even after I started experiencing success, I understood that I should always be in a posture to learn. I sought knowledge from anyone who had it; new agents, agents that I have been around for a long time, etc. I went to a big event for my brokerage firm and some people knew who I was and expected me to act stuck up, but that's not me. You can't grow or behave that way; you have to be open-minded. You have to be willing to learn. This is a constantly changing industry. The market changes every three months, so you have to be flexible and humble to a certain extent.

It's Not So Lonely At The Top

Once you begin building on your foundation, you'll see how your team comes together. There will be some team members that are with you from the very beginning and then leave when it is their time to go. There are team members who joined the mission late, but they're committed to stay as long as they can. You want to be around people that are building you up at the same time as you are building your vision.

People who are willing to wholeheartedly build with you are the type of people that you want to keep alongside you on your journey. You don't want to work with people that are secretly jealous and trying to bring you down like crabs in a barrel. The right team members will bring the best out of you. They will inspire you as you strive to improve.

Though it's a disheartening reminder, I want you to understand that there will be times when you have to make hard decisions regarding your team. Not everyone is meant to go with you. Some team members don't have the same approach and discipline to be in the rooms you will walk in. Some people are only meant to be a part of your journey for a season. There will be instances where you have to let someone go from the team, or try to be supportive when a team member is ready to move on elsewhere. Part of this profession will come with having to learn to let go.

You also have to be mindful that as much as you want to help people, you can't be everything to everyone. You might have an experience where someone close to you seeks to work with you because they need an opportunity. They might be a family member or a really good friend, however, you must analyze their fruit. If they come across as being bad for business, then you probably don't want them for *your business*. I know you love them and want to see them succeed. However, their success should not come at the expense of your dream.

CHECKING YOUR FOUNDATION

I want you to sit back and close your eyes again. How rooted are you in striving for your goals? When was the last time that you had a heart to heart with yourself and what you are trying to do? Have you ever questioned if this was all going to work in the end? On the days where you feel like giving up, keep going. You're going to need to be honest with yourself to determine the direction your business is going in.

How's your heart posture? Are you quick to make impulsive decisions that cost you time, money, and energy? Are you staying true to your why? If you've deviated from your why, what changed? You want to make sure that you're building on solid ground. You don't want to build your dream on the fragility of ego. That's how you get cracks in the foundation. That's how you leave yourself open to people and things that do not benefit your growth in real estate.

A word of advice to you who are known for being very humble, don't be so humble that you fall into low self-esteem. No client is going to want to purchase or sell a home with someone who doesn't feel as though they are confident enough. Don't be overly cocky where you end up turning people off from working with you. Like Andre 3000, keep your heart. Build upwards and build high.

CHAPTER 10

Professionalism As A Realtor

"I think professionalism is important, and professionalism means you get paid."

—*Erica Jong*

Now that we've covered what it takes to build your business from the ground up, I think I would be remiss if we did not address the most crucial aspect of being a realtor: professionalism. I cannot stress how important this factor is because it can make or break you, your business, and your reputation. Before I go into detail about how one ought to be a professional, I believe it's important that we're clear on what professionalism is. It is a word that is thrown around so much that the true meaning gets lost in the mix of corporate jargon.

Professionalism can generally be defined as *"an individual's adherence to a set of standards, code of conduct or collection of qualities that characterize accepted practice within a particular area of activity"* (Universities UK et al. 2004). It can also be defined as *"the skill, good judgment, and polite behavior that is expected from a person who is trained to do a job well"* (Professionalism, n.d.). In other words, professionalism is the way you conduct and present yourself that hopefully reflects the ideals and standard set forth in your respected field. I'm sure many of us can recall a few times where we've dealt with an individual or two who could use a lesson in how to conduct themselves in a professional manner. That being said, let's talk about the 4 areas I believe realtors need to prove themselves professionally.

MAKING A GOOD FIRST IMPRESSION

If I've heard it once, I've heard it a thousand times: "Presentation is everything." How would you feel checking into a five-star hotel and the moment you walk into your room, you find beer cans and bottles strewn about the floor, used towels in the bathroom, and the beds left unmade? Chances are you would never stay at that hotel again after that, right? You might even go as far as leaving a bad review.

Or what if you went to a fine dining establishment where the atmosphere, décor, and service is immaculate, but upon closer examination you find the silverware isn't clean or you find water stains or fingerprints on the glassware? You might give them a pass after the waiter exchanges them for you, but when your meal comes out, you take a bite and much to your displeasure, it is undercooked. Chances are you wouldn't frequent this place again and tell anyone who would listen all about it.

Just as presentation and appearances are important for five-star hotels and restaurants, they are just as important for us realtors. Not only must we look the part when interacting with clients and buyers, but the houses we are looking to sell must be in good condition as well, because your first impression just might be the determinate factor as to whether you land a deal.

BEING KNOWLEDGEABLE

It has been said that you take major risks when you act without knowing what you're doing. This is especially true as a realtor because your knowledge or lack thereof can make or break your chances of closing a deal. So, I suggest that you are well acquainted with whatever knowledge you may need to present. I'm not saying that you must be able to answer every and any question a potential buyer might throw at you, but you should be able to answer the most basic ones.

Once again, life happens – We don't get as much sleep as we would've liked before or we might just draw a blank. It's happened to me, so there is no doubt that it happens to the best of them, too. It's completely fine if you don't know the answer to a question. Simply communicate that you don't have an answer for them at that moment, but you would be glad to either get them an answer or connect them with someone who can provide them with one.

Not only must we be knowledgeable about the information we need to present, but we must also pay close attention to *how* we communicate. Our goal is to communicate in such a way that our clients can understand us clearly and thoroughly.

FOLLOWING A CODE OF CONDUCT

In this industry and beyond, the main code of conduct people operate by is the "Golden Rule," which is to treat others how you would like to be treated. That being said, I am intentional about treating each of my clients with the utmost respect. I strive to be as open and honest as possible with them. I've learned that not only does this build trust, but it is the way to providing them with the best possible experience.

As I said before, my time is valuable and wish for it to be respected. Therefore, I treat my clients' time in the same manner. I make a point to be punctual for all my meetings and appointments. Should I be running late, or need to cancel or reschedule, I communicate that at my earliest convenience.

CREATING A CULTURE OF CUSTOMER SERVICE

Although it is an obvious rule of thumb, I must reiterate that no two clients are the same. It is easy to be in the industry so long that you think you know the ins and outs of who you're selling to so well that you could close the deal with your eyes closed. We must never allow ourselves to become so arrogant to think in such a way, but we instead we must strive to remember that each client is their own person with their own personal set of needs, and it is our job as a realtor to treat them with the utmost dignity and respect as we help them on their journey toward purchasing a home that meets most, if not all their needs. Our clients are people, not numbers. We would not want to be treated as such, so let us not treat them that way.

The best way to ensure that we prioritize our clients, and their needs is by listening to them. Active listening shows the client that they are seen, heard, and ultimately respected. By hearing out their concerns and being able to convey a working solution, we show the client that we are trustworthy and that they can have confidence that we are putting their interests above our own. Although business and logistics play a major role in our dealings with clients, we must never limit ourselves to those aspects alone. We must take special care to appeal to their humanity, get to the root of why they're interested or not interested in a home, and determine how we can help them along. At its core, professionalism is a fine balance of the knowledge of the facts you're presenting, and the knowledge of the people you're serving.

CHAPTER 11

How To Conduct A Home Inspection

"To be successful in real estate, you must always and consistently put your clients' best interests first. When you do, your personal needs will be realized beyond your greatest expectations."

—*Anthony Hitt*

Anyone that has purchased or has thought about purchasing a home, has heard the term home inspection. However, many people may not understand the importance of a home inspection being done. There are a plethora of reasons to inspect a home that benefit both buyer and seller. So, allow me to give you a brief synopsis.

Home inspectors can honestly be one of the best pre-home buying strategies a home buyer can use. They can alleviate any risks by ensuring everything in the house is in buying condition. A home inspector can give you an honest picture of the entire building and help you to understand where your money truly is going. Before hiring a home inspector, do this quick inspection yourself to see if this house is worth that next step.

WALLS, FLOORS, AND CEILINGS

The walls, floors, and ceilings are the biggest areas to check for water damage and mold. If you see any water damage or even discolored spots in your walls, ceiling, or flooring, you should take that as a sign of caution. Any visible water damage could mean serious problems within the walls, and even with your insulation. One of the issues that water damage can lead to is the formation of unhealthy, black mold. This can affect the health of the clients in a negative way and can be possible grounds for a lawsuit if not properly taken care of. If you see any damage, that will mean a hefty inspection and quite a bit of repair until that space is livable.

ELECTRICAL

Typically, people will check the electrical system by switching lights on and off since that seems to be the most reasonable way to check for any issues. But one thing you can particularly keep an eye out for is the electrical outlets and switches. If they look brand new, sometimes that could mean the room was recently wired. If that's the case, you may want to check the outlets with a receptacle tester to make sure everything was wired correctly. If it wasn't wired correctly, it could mean the homeowner tried to fix the wiring themselves. Failure to properly maintain the electrical system could increase the likeliness of the home catching on fire. Should that scenario present itself, it would mean an even greater risk to the buyer purchasing the home.

FURNACE

The biggest thing you can do is check the age of the furnace. A furnace's life span is around 20-25 years, and a well-maintained furnace can last up to 30 or 40 years. Make sure to check the date of the furnace to see how long it's been running by looking for stickers that document routine service. Another reason to check the furnace is because like the electrical in the home, it can pose a danger by being a fire hazard. If a furnace isn't properly serviced, it can lead to potentially dangerous issues.

BASEMENT

Along with leaky roofs and other sources for water problems, the basement can experience a few water problems of its own. Basement water damage can come from two sources: indoor humidity condensing on cold surfaces, and water coming in from the outside.

If it's from the outside that means the drainage system may not be set up well for the house. If you see water damage in the basement, you will want to check where it's coming from. You can diagnose the water problem by doing this.

OTHER POTENTIAL ISSUES

While conducting a home inspection, keep an eye out for things like ants, roaches, and termites. Ants and roaches can affect the quality of living in a space. Termites affect the quality of living and the condition of the home by the effect the have on the wood within. Also look for things like rat and mouse droppings. Should any of these signs be found, contact pest control immediately to handle the problem as it is easier to handle those problems when the property is vacant.

THE BENEFITS OF HOME INSPECTION

A home inspection helps you make a more informed decision about the home you're considering buying. A home inspector can identify potential issues, plus give you a better idea of the ongoing maintenance the property will require. The goal of a home inspection is to uncover issues with the home itself. Inspectors won't tell you if you're getting a good deal on the home or offer an opinion on the sale price.

A home inspection can also affect the sale of a home. We'll take a look at why a seller needs a home inspection in a moment. Pop quiz! Why does a home inspection affect the sale of a home? Think about it. You got it! It can help determine the asking price of the home being sold. Imagine a seller is listing a house for $500,000, and they receive a viable offer. Everything looks great, the seller is selling, the buyer is getting a great home. Everyone is excited. But then, after the home inspection is done, and it is revealed that there is a termite infestation, or severe water damage, this sale and purchase of the home can be halted.

A home inspection is not just about the cosmetics of a home, you know the pretty stuff. It is about what is underneath the hood. Just like when you purchase the car of your dreams, it looks beautiful, everything you've ever wanted but what is under the hood? Is the engine good, is the carburetor in good working condition, and what about the brake pads? This is the same concept of a home inspection. You must look beyond the surface to see what is really happening.

WHAT DOES AN INSPECTION ENTAIL?

Inspectors should begin by walking outside, around the property and inspecting the exterior which allows them to notice and make note of any issues or concerns that could also affect the inside of the home. The roof and the garage should be inspected next before going inside the property. Keep in mind that something of concern on the outside can affect the inside.

As the inspection goes into the home the process starts upstairs in the attic and eventually leads to the basement. The basement is saved for last because if there are leaks discovered with the plumbing inside the home, this allows for any drips to be noticed by the time the inspector gets to the basement. Every room in the home is inspected for electrical problems, and any problems with the heating and cooling systems.

A good home inspection should take several hours. It should include checklists, pictures and notes. The critical information should include recommended repairs and replacements. An inspection is not a pass-fail exam. No fixes are mandatory after a home inspection, though it may uncover issues that prompt further negotiations with the seller. You'll learn much about the home and gain confidence in the decision to move into your new address — or find out enough to pass on the purchase. Remember these tips:

Parts of the home that are commonly included in a home inspection:

- Structural components (floors, walls, ceilings, stairs).

- Exterior components (siding, attached decks, porches).
- Roof.
- Plumbing.
- Heating and air conditioning.
- Major appliances.
- Ventilation.
- Insulation.
- Fireplaces and wood stoves.
- Windows and doors.

It's important for real estate agents to understand home inspection basics, as it's a key part of the home purchase process. So, does the realtor go to the home inspection? Yes, you should attend the inspection. You will spend plenty of time reading through inspection reports with your clients, as they will want to know your opinion of the inspector's findings. By knowing what a home inspector is required and not required to report on, you will be able to advise your clients during negotiations and help them get their next home at a fair price.

Understanding the home inspection process can give you a leg up on your competition, and make your clients feel more at ease because you'll have insider knowledge on what went on during the inspection.

Valuable Tip: Require your clients to attend the home inspection at least for the last 45 minutes if they cannot stay the entire time. However, before everyone leaves force the inspector to give the clients a summary of what's going to be on the report because it is; less daunting then the client reading the issues alone later. Sometimes small issues can cause clients to panic just because they don't fully understand the issue, but if it's properly explained to them, they can make a more informed decision about how to properly get it fixed.

CHAPTER 12

How To Attract Business With Your Attire

"Clothes and manners do not make the man; but, when he is made, they greatly improve his appearance."

—*Henry Ward Beecher*

We have all the heard the mantra, "dress for success." This is true, we have to dress for the role we are in. But this is more than just putting on a suit and tie. When you look good, and you know that you look good, you feel good. That translates to how confident you are. That confidence along with the suit and tie is what your clients need to see. Never underestimate the power of your image.

My mentor, Jason, taught me that dressing correctly is as important as having knowledge. When you show up, you have to show up correctly. That means your shirt is crispy and not wrinkled. Shoes are shined, there are no buttons missing, no stains on your tie or your jacket. You get my point. You dress with confidence, talk with confidence, and walk with confidence. All of this helps your clients to trust you.

Your look can convey and imply a huge amount of information about your business, such as your professionalism, quality, friendliness, and values. It can also help to instill confidence in your brand and products.

THE POWER OF PERCEPTION

Think about this analogy. If you went to a laundromat to wash your clothes, and the laundromat was dirty, would you trust washing your clothes there? Absolutely not. When you go out to the store , and you can tell moths have gotten to the clothes, you are not going to want to spend your money there, and definitely not purchase any clothing items from them.

Perception is important. Your clients need to see a professional well-dressed agent that they can trust to work with them. Without realizing it, your image displays that you have their best interest in mind. If your appearance says you don't care about yourself, what will make your clients think that you care about them?

You also need to be prepared for meeting and working with your clients. Whether the meeting is online or in person, do your homework do your homework. You can wear a great suit and be dressed for success and not be able to articulate the facts. It is all about confidence, confidence, and more confidence. That confidence can only come from being prepared.

CLOTHES MAKE THE MAN

George Horace Lorimer once said, "Clothes don't make the man, but they make all of him except his hands and face during business hours, and that's a pretty considerable area of the human mammal." Follow that up with the quote above from Henry Ward Beecher, "Clothes and manners do not make the man; but, when he is made, they greatly improve his appearance." What you wear during your business hours has an impact. What you're wearing helps to improve your impact. As the quote above says, "Clothes and manners do not make the man; but, when he is made, they greatly approve his appearance, "but when he is made.", you have to determine when you are made. Have you put in the work to make yourself ready to show your best self?

Anyone that you do business with should always meet the best you. Before you leave out of the house or the office for a meeting look in the mirror and ask yourself what you see. If you question what you see, start over.

Disclaimer: I know several realtors that dress casually all the time, however as a 23-year-old African

American realtor it was important for me to show up as the best version of myself at all times. Therefore, clothing is imperative to me.

CLOSING

Ladies and gentlemen, we've reached the end of the Twelve Points journey. It is my hope that these points will be a guide for you on your journey. I'm extremely grateful that you would add this book to your toolkit of being a successful real estate agent. When things get rough on your journey, may you revisit this book for encouragement and wisdom.

I once again charge you to use your position in the real estate industry to help change the world in your own unique way. Shoot for the stars but aim for the moon. Let your goals and aspirations propel you forward, and don't be afraid to revisit them later and dream bigger. Connect with your clients in authenticity. Do not covet the journeys and experiences of other realtors as their journeys will not grow you in the way that yours will.

Give it your all in all that you do. I believe that as you seek out God's plan for your life that you will see Him work miracles within the work that you do. Do not be discouraged if no one is cheering for you. He's always in your corner. Other than Him, your biggest advocate is you. Do not forget that.

I sincerely wish you the best on your real estate journey. I wish you much success in your journey. I also encourage you to pay it forward and that you share this book with others who are just starting their journey. I want to help as many people as possible. I want people to see that they can build a legacy for themselves through real estate. I want people to see what is possible when they focus and work diligently.

Real estate is an investment that can lead to financial freedom. As you are growing in knowledge in this area, I encourage you to seek wisdom as changes are made in the industry. If you keep yourself educated, you will rarely be caught off guard by the ebbs and flows of the industry. Do not grow weary in well doing. The inspiration is there, do not be afraid to strike the iron while it is hot. I thank you again for choosing this book as a resource and wish that you will continue to follow me on my journey. There's more to come.

Montaz McCray